HOME SERIES

HOME SERIES
COSY LIVING

BETA-PLUS

CONTENTS

P. 4-5
Chris van Eldik and Wendy
Jansen's house doubles up
as a showroom for their JOB
furniture collection.

P. 6
A Vlassak Verhulst creation in
Hamburg using lime paints.
The oak floor is supplied by
Corvelyn.

INTRODUCTION

olour is a language and a means of expression for cosy living. It plays a pivotal role in the style of an interior as it creates atmosphere, evokes trends, conveys feelings and creates ambiance. However, depending on the materials with which they are used, colours may reveal different intensities or convey different meanings. When applied to a gloss surface, they may suddenly seem precious, whilst combined with a matt texture, they may appear more soothing.

Nowadays, innovation, diversity and illusion are the watchwords in all aspects of furnishing and decorating your interior from the floor through to the ceiling. There are a vast array of new materials and paints to choose from. Do you opt for wood floors or imitation wood floors? How about fabric or wallpaper? Should it be concrete or a paint effect? There is also no shortage of fabrics, offering a wide variety of textures and materials which may be silky, coarse, smooth, crumpled or metallic.

A plethora of new materials such as the synthetic resins Corian, Solid Surface and Cristalplant have enabled shapes to be designed which were previously not possible and are supplementing or replacing enamelled porcelain, acrylic, glass, terracotta, stainless steel and natural stone. Innovations have also been made with natural materials, allowing them to take centre stage once again. For example, wooden floors are back in vogue thanks to floating floors and exotic wood types such as teak, Ipê and Merbeau.

In this publication, you will discover a lot of examples of "cosy living", both modern and authentic, all expertly displayed in breathtaking interiors.

P. 8
An Odile and Virginie Dejaegere creation.

P. 10-11
This living room in a country home was designed by Lionel Jadot.

MINIMALIST, CLASSIC AND CHIC

C hris Van Eldik and Wendy Jansen set up as interior designers about ten years ago in the Dutch town of Wijk bij Duurstede.

Their style may be described as 'classic minimalist': warm, natural, authentic and untreated materials placed in staunchly modern surroundings with a hint of minimalism.

They are pioneers of untreated lime paints which have become fashionable in recent years and their penchant for this finish is in perfect keeping with an overall effect which is timeless, simple and intimate.

Chris and Wendy also produce their own collection of furniture under the JOB Intérieur brand. In this feature, they invite you to take a look at their showroom and private house which are both effortlessly elegant and defy passing trends.

View of the chapel: a 1.5-seat Huygen linen armchair with removable covers, an oak block on a cow hide rug and silk curtains in the background.

On the left, two Job 10 dining room benches and a footrest covered with a black cow hide. On top is a metal tray with hand blown glassware. Painting by Christiaan Lieverse.

P.16-17
A Huygen sofa measuring 280cm in width with a natural-coloured linen cover. 1.5-seat Huygen armchair. On the right, a padded footrest and dining room bench (Job 10) covered in a dark rubberized fabric. Silver silk curtains. Modular lighting.

Note...

> Behind the simple appearance, the harmony of monochrome colours is enriched and intensified by the diversity of the materials and textures used. The matt finish goes hand in hand with the satin and the linen complements the silk. Here simplicity rubs shoulders with luxury.

> Padded seats are back with a vengeance.

Some samples from the Job collection – a dark grey linen corner sofa and a Job 10 dining room bench with a low padded rubber back.

Lodewijk model in dark grey cotton.
Aubergine lime paint applied to the walls.
Green-mauve shiny acetate curtains.

Decoration idea

> The lime "livens up" the walls by creating different shades and effects which are accentuated by a muted and deep colour. When set off against silky curtains, this heightens the sense of mystery.

Oak flooring has been used on the mezzanine floor. The left hand page shows a natural linen Lodewijk armchair. The fireplace has been meticulously restored. Lime paint has been applied to the walls and Modular lighting installed. Above and opposite are two silver-grey dining room benches around an antique painted double desk. In the foreground are some black linen corner seats.

P.22-23

The original back room which has been converted into a living room is furnished with fitted cupboards. The room features a Huygen settee, two Stijn armchairs and a long coffee table made of reclaimed wood. The chandelier was produced in black by Van Brand and Van Egmond at the owners' request. Grey lime paint has been used on the walls and cupboards.

Decoration idea

> The black cow hide rug mirrors the dark ceiling. This silky rug is a designer item and contrasts beautifully with the rustic floor.

> (p 22-23) A serene and understated room with monochrome colours enhanced by the variety of materials used.

Pink lime paint has been used to paint this little girl's bedroom.

Son Olivier's bedroom features bleached wooden wardrobes, a green velvet Ewout armchair and a white ceiling.

The bed with its Society cover is part of the Job collection. In the foreground is a linen footrest with antique legs. Émile armchair and standing lamp.

A SUBTLE TRANSFORMATION

nterior designer Francis Luy-paert took a subtle approach to refurbishing this house. By making a few small changes and adding a sophisticated selection of furniture, in close consultation with the owner of the property, he has given the living room a whole new appearance.

A colour scheme of white, beige, oatmeal, taupe and black gives the room an airy and relaxed feel. The colours combine to produce timeless elegance.

Francis Luypaert helped the owner of this house to choose the furniture, including Minotti armchairs, a Club B&B Italia coffee table and armchairs (Maxalto collection) and a leather rug.

Note...

> Wood in all its guises from light oak, to wenge, to bleached wood. The material is used throughout and adds a great deal of warmth.

> In this large space, the rug marks out the living room area and creates a cosy nook.

The fireplace has been kept and given a more invigorating colour.

Maxalto table and chairs with oatmeal
leather cushions.

P.30-31
Full view of the living room.

The colours of the lampshades were selected with meticulous attention to detail.
Table from Maxalto. The industrial cooker hood is fully integrated into the ceiling.

Decoration idea

> There is a touch of humour in the kitchen with the two giant bright green pears. This invigorating dash of colour adds freshness and dynamism to a room in which wenge dominates.

P.32
Untreated matt ceramic tiles cover the floor. The furniture is made of a laminated oak combination with a horizontal decorative pattern.

The overall effect is accentuated by in-built and indirect lighting. The floor has been treated and a semi-matt varnish has been applied. The furniture is made of a selection of vertically laminated Oregon pine, which has been brushed, dyed and painted with matt varnish. Linen blinds.

Note...

> Warmer and more homely colours are used in the en-suite area, creating a more friendly and authentic atmosphere.

The same laminated Oregon pine finish is used in the bathroom. The sink is clad in natural Moleanos stone. Indirect LED lighting has been fitted in the space behind the bathtub.

FACELIFT FOR A MODERN COTTAGE

nterior designer Isabelle Bijvoet has transformed this cottage.

The open-plan living area (and its lowered lounge) has been given a facelift.

Durable materials, a lack of clutter and warm colours create a simple yet homely overall effect.

The striped Jules Flipo carpet perfectly matches the wenge furniture.

Bijvoet believes that synergy is of utmost importance and by collaborating with the owners, she has created an interior in which everyone feels at home. The aim was to keep some of the original materials and combine them with more contemporary elements.

Decoration idea

> The concealed neon lighting under the upper part of the television wall transmits gentle light and illuminates the casing.

> The vertical frames balance out the three horizontal levels (the lower storage area, the plasma screen and the row of paintings).

> Offsetting flooring with fashionable and retro designs against simple décor, natural colours and light furniture avoids overloading the overall effect.

Linen curtains and bedding.
Grooved and varnished MDF cupboards
and panelling.

Decoration idea

> Resting paintings on the
headboard means you can
change them whenever you
feel like it.

> The sink area is concealed
in a cupboard (p 43).

> Classic materials used in
an original way – the oak
flooring is laid in a square
pattern (p 43).

The master bedroom and its simple, stylish dressing room in which natural materials have been used. Varnished wenge and MDF cupboards and wall panelling. Linen curtains by Domus Vivendi.

A MODERN COUNTRY HOUSE

WITH A TOUCH OF NOSTALGIA

Although it has only recently been built, the country house in this feature gives the illusion of age.

This illusion is not only created by the consistent use of weather-beaten reclaimed materials for the exterior. The interior also radiates a timeless atmosphere steeped in history.

Dankers Decor, one of the most famous decorating companies in Belgium and a longstanding supplier to the court, has created a harmony of colours throughout the house. It has used Arte Constructo mineral lime paints coloured with natural pigments to create a tailored solution for an extraordinary dwelling.

Most of the pieces of antique furniture are family heirlooms passed down from generation to generation.

Note...

> Very stylish loose-hanging taffeta curtains (allow at least 20cm excess) provide a theatrical effect.

> Treated and bleached wood panelling lighten the décor.

Antique Carrara marble floor tiles.

The fitted oak cupboards have been
treated with mineral lime. La Cornue
stove in the centre has two vaulted ovens.

The walls of the swimming pool area have been coated in plaster and lime by Dankers Decor.

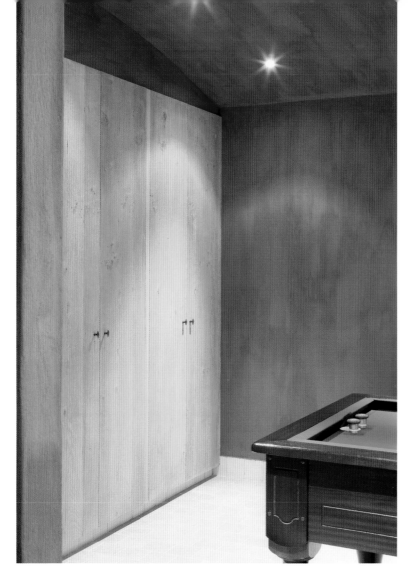

The orange shade seen in this room was produced from a mixture of Arte Constructo mineral lime and ground iron oxide.

Here, Dankers Decor has combined casein limewash with oxide green. The fine silk curtains were hand-embroidered in Italy.

The cupboards in the dressing room have been treated.

Old cheese racks have been used for the flooring.

THE ETERNAL BEAUTY OF STONE

Themenos has refurbished the interior of this large country house in its timeless and relaxed style.

Van den Weghe (The Stonecompany) has provided a tailored solution using natural stone. A wide variety of materials can be seen in the building including bricks, slate and cement tiles. This eclectic approach gives the house its charm.

View towards the kitchen. The bricks used for the floor were supplied by Rik Storms.

The small kitchen features several types of aged Burgundy marble and white stone. Bluestone work surfaces and block sink with moulded finish.

Beaten bluestone briquettes are used on the floor.

Sculpted bluestone block wash basin in the basement.

Note...

> The patchwork flooring in the kitchen livens up the room.

> This slate floor has been laid in an original way, copying the chevron formation often used for parquet.

> Bricks are laid upright, a time-honoured technique which makes floors more hardwearing.

Two hand-carved block sinks in bluestone (left hand page) and in Marron Emperador, a type of Spanish marble (above).
Gris Cehigin (flambé finish), another type of Spanish stone, has been used on the floor. Created by Themenos.

A SEASIDE APARTMENT

WITH RUSTIC CHARM

T he leitmotiv for this apartment in Knokke-le-Zoute was devised by Vera Dankers on behalf of Dankers Creation.

She took overall responsibility for material furnishings (curtains and fabrics) and selecting the furniture.

Dankers Decor was commissioned to paint the apartment using Arte Constructo products, which it applied in original ways.

Dankers Decor used a mineral painting technique which superimposes several thin layers of patina. The artworks are by Jef Verheyen (left hand page) and Renaat Ivens (above).

Decoration idea

> It's not concrete! Oatmeal-coloured lime has been used to create this contemporary-looking floor. Combined with the rustic pieces of furniture, it adds a subtle modern touch to a style otherwise reminiscent of the countryside.

P.60-61
A protective layer of oil-based paint has been applied to the lime-based flooring designed by Dankers Decor.
This process has a number of benefits: it uses a natural product (mineral lime), limed flooring can be laid on an existing mineral surface and only between 5mm and 2cm maximum in height is lost when it is laid.
The prewashed Italian linen curtains were produced by Dankers Creation.

The same flooring used in the rest of the apartment is also found in the bathroom. The edge of the bathtub and the walls have been coated in tadelakt, which is a waterproof coating.

Cotton and linen curtains with antique pink and grey stripes.
The beds and bedding were also supplied by Dankers Creation.

A LISTED BUILDING REFURBISHED

IN MINIMALIST STYLE

This house, built in 1807, once belonged to a notary and both the facades and interior are listed. The main body of this majestic residence has the feel of a house owned by someone of standing.

Its adjoining rooms have a rustic feel and blend seamlessly into the rest of the building. Their design was entrusted to architect Stéphane Boens.

This refurbishment is based on two guiding principles – authenticity and simplicity. It therefore comes as no surprise that white has been chosen as the main colour as it accentuates the purity and beauty of the building.

Furniture and objects have been used to add colour and are set off against the simple backdrop to create a sort of minimalist effect which is in harmony with the antique materials. The owners have been working with Stéphane Boens for several years, a collaboration which has proven very fruitful and has enabled them to perfect the refurbishment of their home. All the painting was carried out by Frank Verschuere and most of the furniture was supplied by am projects.

An old church floor has been laid in the entrance hall of the notary's house. The walls have been painted with white lime using a time-honoured method. The chandelier is new but has been designed based on an old Louis XV model. The original staircase and double door lead to the garden and let in the surrounding countryside.

The entrance leads to the kitchen via the laundry room.
The wardrobe in the cloakroom is made of reclaimed oak doors which have been painted white.
The doors to the laundry room are also reclaimed oak doors to which the same technique has been applied. The floor tiles are old flagstones from a church. The 'antique red' front door provides the sole hint of colour. A Thomas Huyghe painting hangs above the red-brown Spanish bench (am projects).

Decoration idea

> The floor and staircase in the entrance hall are accentuated by the immaculate white of the walls. This is an effective method for modernising the interior.

> The red door at the end of the corridor accentuates perspective and adds dynamism to the colour scheme.

The original decorative plasterwork ceiling in this living room has been restored by Frank Verschuere. The walls have been painted with household lime paint and given a clay finish. Oak interior shutters, Axel Vervoordt seating and an aged oak floor.

The entire kitchen has been covered in Dutch witjes tiles.

The floor is an old cement floor which has been restored.

A white AGA stove and antique Provencal chairs are combined with a set of 18th century chairs (am projects). The wood panelling conceals a staircase which leads to the attic housing the children's games room.

The antique oak table with integrated electrical sockets can be used both as a dining room table and a desk.

White lime paint has been used in the dining room. The chandelier dates back to the late 18th century. The Spanish walnut table is also from the 18th century (am projects) and the antique pink wardrobe has been restored to its original condition by Frank Verschuere. To the left of the pink wardrobe are three children's drawings. Aged oak flooring.

White lime paint has also been used in the family room. The wardrobe next to the open fire is made of reclaimed door panels. Several layers of household paint have been applied to create an aged look. Armchairs by am projects. Aged oak floor.

The fitted bathtub has wood panelling. The surround is matt white marble and the flooring is reclaimed white marble. The antique black cabinet is from the Netherlands.

In the hallway leading to the bedrooms and bathroom, there is an 18th century brown-red Spanish bench. Reclaimed pitch pine has been used on the floors. The walk-in wardrobe has been made to measure but, like the cabinet, has kept its original doors. Several layers of white paint have been applied to these. The only hint of colour in this dressing room is provided by the red chandelier. Reclaimed pitch pine has been used on the floors.

The two children's rooms in the attic have been refurbished. White lime paint has been used on the walls and beams in Cesar's bedroom.

Several layers of lime (blue-green) have been applied to the antique bed to give it an aged look.

White lime paint has also been used on the walls and beams of Lea's bedroom.

The little antique bed has also been painted antique pink using the same method used on her brother's bed.

MOMENTS OF REFLECTION

Interior designers Tiene Lauren and Frank Tahon from ZONE-dertig are responsible for the two projects in this feature. Their designs are pure, timeless and espouse a 'no-nonsense' approach, using straight lines and concepts which create harmony.

The overall effect radiates minimalism and inner peace.

The wide and highly attractive corridor in this centre for therapeutic meditation with its twinson decking and multi-purpose white units leads directly to the vast space behind the building via the patio.

Decked out in white from its wooden floor to the ceiling, this old ironworks has been converted into a magnificent space. The splash of purple adds another dimension as it represents the seventh chakra which is associated with spirituality.

Note...

> Repetition is an easy way of creating a deco effect. Here, an original suspended sculpture has been produced simply by clustering paper light shades.

The kitchen shown here is part of a private residence. The touch of black provided by the suspended unit made of fibre board and black granite contrasts with the white kitchen wall which is made of fibre board and Corian. The L-shaped stainless steel surface with its integrated hotplate forms a clear and open boundary between the cooking area and the dining room.

The high wall of cupboards links the living rooms to the bedrooms without partitioning them off and provides a welcoming open-plan layout. This connecting wall with satin varnish finish also provides discreet access to the cloakroom, toilet, bathroom, laundry room and bedrooms.

The black suspended kitchen unit combines a black textured varnish finish with a composite stone work surface. Behind the hotplates is a white enamelled glass wall.

Note...

> The flat screen television nestled in the partition wall is both minimalist and decorative.

> Warmth is given to this minimalist space by the flooring with its warm shades.

> Concealed lighting brightens up the suspended units.

A COUNTRY HOME

WITH CHARACTER

This charming property has been completely refurbished by Alain and Brigitte Garnier in a style which is both casual and sophisticated.

Verraes was responsible for painting the house. A timeless rustic style has been chosen for this homely abode. Extreme restraint has been shown in terms of the décor with furniture and coverings combining to create perfect harmony, primarily through colour – beige is dominant throughout the interior.

An open oak bookshelf designed and produced by Garnier.
The slightly crumpled C&C linen curtains were produced and hung by Garnier.

An 18th century Italian walnut seat upholstered with de Le Cuona fabric. The curtains were produced using Le Manach fabric by Garnier.
The lantern dates back to around 1800. All the other lights were made in Belgium and are available from Garnier.

Decoration idea

> Combine curtains and shutters – curtains are decorative and shutters are functional.

French terracotta floor tiles and black Moroccan zellige wall tiles are found in the kitchen. The candle chandelier is made of wrought iron and the blinds were produced by Garnier using Le Manach fabric.

P.98-99
An 18th century French dresser with its original marble. An Italian table with small-scale English chairs. A set of china candleholders.

Chaise longue with white linen cover. 18th century Italian trestle table with walnut armchair. 18th century varnished French chest of draws. Chelsea Textiles bedspread and C&C curtains, Garnier design and fabrics.

CREATING A MODERN SPACE

WITH LIME PAINT

The company Arte Constructo based in Schelle has made a name for itself within the renovation industry as an international supplier of mineral, natural and organic products such as Unilit (natural hydraulic lime), Coridecor (immaculate lime putty-based finish) and Keim (silicate paints). It is also famous for its quality mortar.

An immaculate lime putty-based finish can be achieved using the Coridecor range. The range includes products such as Corical (lime paint), Marmolux and Coristil (marbled finish), Venestuk (Venetian stucco) and Decorlux (smooth and glossy finish). These lime-based products have antiallergenic and disinfectant properties.

Coridecor products can be applied to very interesting effect in a modern and timeless interior as illustrated by this feature on a house on the Belgian coast, which has been painted from top to bottom by the firm de Waal using Corical products.

Decoration idea

> Lighting effects – an expertly placed ceiling light is all that is required to create a beautiful décor and offers a visually stunning focus for the entrance hall. In the background, a statue bathed in light creates an air of mystery.

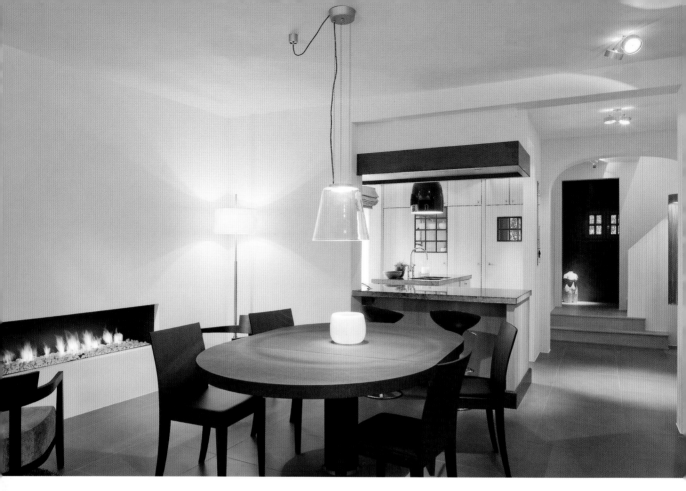

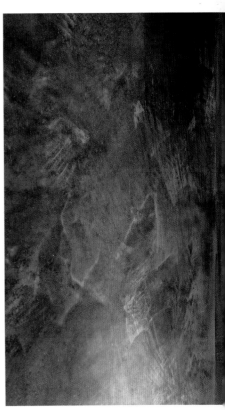

A homely and elegant kitchen which uses wood throughout. The work surface and the large ceiling light complement the picture window.

Decoration idea

> Painting window frames in black creates an interesting decorative effect whereby attention is drawn to the exterior.

Gentle colours have been used in this cosy bathroom adjoining the bedroom.
An industrial touch is provided by the large glazed partition.

A host of gentle taupe shades are used on the floor. This combined with the coral red-tinctured walls of the staircase creates a very effective harmony of colours.

A small display on the landing: a large mirror and two pieces of pottery are all it takes to create a serene space.

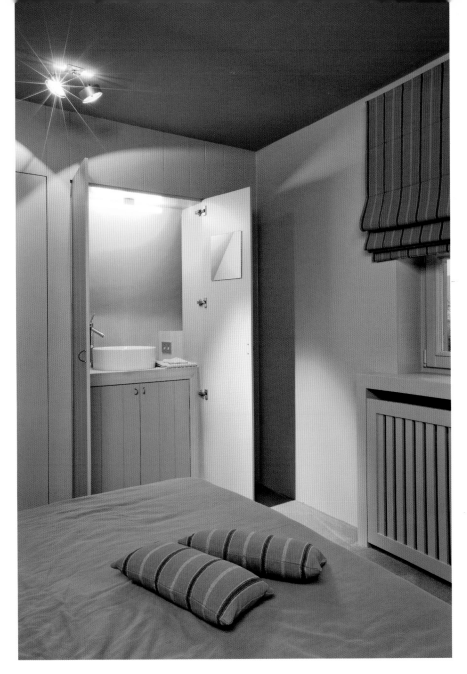

The same combination of taupe and livelier colours is found in the bedrooms. These colours instantly create a cosy and intimate atmosphere.

HOME SERIES

Volume 26 : COSY LIVING

The reports in this book are selected from the Beta-Plus collection of home-design books: www.betaplus.com
They have been compiled in a special series by Le Figaro in French language: Ma Déco.

Copyright © 2010 Beta-Plus Publishing / Le Figaro
Originally published in French language

PUBLISHER
Beta-Plus Publishing
Termuninck 3
B – 7850 Enghien
Belgium
www.betaplus.com
info@betaplus.com

TEXT
Alexandra Druesne

PHOTOGRAPHY
Jo Pauwels

DESIGN
Polydem - Nathalie Binart

TRANSLATIONS
Txt-Ibis

ISBN : 978-90-8944-080-8

Printed in China

P.122-123
A Francis Luypaert creation.

P.124-125
An open-plan kitchen/living room designed by FilipTackdesignoffice
The breakfast bar was designed by the natural stone company Van den Weghe.

P.126-127
A living room designed by interior designer Isabelle Bijvoet.